2 - 2/2013 · 5/13

OCEAN ENGINEERING
AND Designing for the Deep Sea

Crabtree Publishing Company

www.crabtreebooks.com

Rebecca Sjonger

Crabtree Publishing Company

www.crabtreebooks.com

Author: Rebecca Sjonger

Series research and development: Reagan Miller

Editorial director: Kathy Middleton

Photo research: James Nixon

Editors: Paul Humphrey, James Nixon, and Philip Gebhardt

Proofreader: Wendy Scavuzzo

Layout: sprout.uk.com

Cover design and logo: Margaret Amy Salter

Production coordinator and prepress technician: Margaret Amy Salter

Print coordinator: Katherine Berti

Consultant: Carolyn de Cristofano, M.Ed. STEM consultant, Professional Development Director of Engineering is Elementary (2005–2008)

Production coordinated by Discovery Books

Photographs:
Alamy: pp. 9 bottom (Washington Imaging), 14 (Rob Arnold), 28 bottom (Design Pics Inc).
Bigstock: pp. 8 (Mana Photo), 13 top (designua), 18 (Ammentorp), 21 middle (gemenacom), 21 bottom (Yommy).
Getty Images: pp. 4 (Danita Delimont), 11 (Darryl Leniuk), 15 (TORSTEN BLACKWOOD/AFP), 17 (Brian Skerry/National Geographic).
NOAA: pp. 9 middle (Bonaire 2008: Exploring Coral Reef Sustainability with New Technologies expedition), 16 (C. Martinez), 23 top (Submarine Ring of Fire 2002/OER).
Wikimedia: pp. 5 top (NASA/Kathryn Hansen), 6 (NOAA), 7 top (NOAA), 9 top (NASA/JPL), p10 top (NOAA Okeanos Explorer Program, Galapagos Rift Expedition 2011), 12 top, 12 bottom (NOAA Ship Collection), 13 bottom (U.S. Navy), 23 bottom (NOAA National Estuarine Research Reserve Collection), 24 (Submarine Ring of Fire 2006 Exploration, NOAA Vents Program), 27 (Mass Communication Specialist 1st Class Dustin Kelling), 28 top (P123), 28 bottom (Van.takacs), 29 bottom (US Bureau of Ocean Energy Management).
Woods Hole Oceanographic Institution: pp. 10 bottom (James Dunn), 19 (Tom Kleindinst), 21 top (Tom Kleindinst), 22 (Tom Kleindinst), 25 (Dana Yoerger).

Library and Archives Canada Cataloguing in Publication

Sjonger, Rebecca, author
   Ocean engineering and designing for the deep sea / Rebecca Sjonger.

(Engineering in action)
Includes index.
Issued in print and electronic formats.
ISBN 978-0-7787-7536-2 (hardback).--ISBN 978-0-7787-7540-9 (paperback).--ISBN 978-1-4271-1785-4 (html)

    1. Ocean engineering--Juvenile literature. I. Title. II. Series: Engineering in action (St. Catharines, Ont.)

TC1645 S56 2016   j620'.4162   C2016-903290-6
                                             C2016-903291-4

Library of Congress Cataloging-in-Publication Data

CIP available at the Library of Congress

Crabtree Publishing Company

www.crabtreebooks.com   1-800-387-7650

Printed in Canada/072016/EF20160630

Published in Canada
Crabtree Publishing
616 Welland Ave.
St. Catharines, ON
L2M 5V6

Published in the United States
Crabtree Publishing
PMB 59051
350 Fifth Avenue, 59th Floor
New York, New York 10118

Published in the United Kingdom
Crabtree Publishing
Maritime House
Basin Road North, Hove
BN41 1WR

Published in Australia
Crabtree Publishing
3 Charles Street
Coburg North
VIC, 3058

CONTENTS

WHAT IS OCEAN ENGINEERING?

Working in oceans comes with many challenges. The waters are deep and often far from land. Humans cannot survive in great depths without help. Ocean engineers solve these problems. They design **technologies** to help people explore and benefit from oceans. We know more about how Earth formed, climate change, and marine life, thanks to ocean engineering solutions. These include imaging **sensors** that monitor ocean environments, robotic vessels that work at different depths, and offshore structures.

EIGHT STEPS TO SUCCESS

The design process is a series of steps. Ocean engineers follow them to develop, build, and test solutions for working in the deep sea. Engineers may focus on one or more steps in the design process.

This mini submarine helps people explore marine life on a coral reef.

Steps in the design process

Define the problem
↓
Identify criteria and constraints
↓
Brainstorm ideas
↓
Select a solution
↓
Build a prototype
↓
Test the prototype
↓
Improve the design
↓
Share the solution

Engineers and scientists : Ocean engineers work with scientists called oceanographers. These scientists study the animals, materials, and processes found in oceans. Engineers use their understanding of oceans to come up with solutions that allow scientists to do their research. For example, ocean engineers find ways to study conditions in remote areas of oceans. They develop tools that measure and collect data. These tools attach to **buoys** designed to float on the ocean's surface. Adding a device that sends the data allows scientists to observe the conditions from land.

This buoy helped scientists study changes in the Arctic Ocean.

Dr. Moran told Seaside Magazine what she loves about ocean engineering "is the fact you can take practical tools and apply them to important ocean science problems."

DR. KATE MORAN

Canadian-American Dr. Kate Moran leads Ocean Networks Canada. It runs **observatories** in the Pacific Ocean off the coast of British Columbia. Dr. Moran was introduced to ocean engineering by her schoolteacher. The subject combined her interest in oceans, science, and math. Dr. Moran went on to become an expert ocean engineer. She led the first team to investigate the underwater earthquake that caused the Indian Ocean **tsunami** in 2004. Dr. Moran has also advised the United States government on issues related to oceans. In 2010, her team came up with solutions after a deep-water drilling disaster in the Gulf of Mexico caused massive damage to marine life. They suggested ways to stop the flow of oil into the ocean and prevent further harm.

ZONES AND LANDFORMS

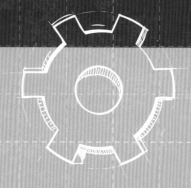

Five connected oceans cover more than two thirds of the planet. Did you know they contain most of Earth's life forms? They also have about 97 percent of the planet's water. The oceans are vital to human survival. These global waters affect climates. They hold natural resources and information about Earth's materials and processes. However, most of the oceans remain unexplored. Technologies designed by ocean engineers help humans discover more about ocean waters and landforms.

Studying the seafloor: Some scientists research how Earth formed by studying landforms on the seafloor. Earth's top layers—called the crust and the upper mantle—divide into massive **tectonic plates** that cover the planet. Thermal energy, or heat, from inside Earth shifts them very slowly. As they move, **magma** escapes through the plate boundaries. The magma builds up over time to form underwater mountain chains called mid-ocean ridges.

When sea water seeps through cracks in the surrounding crust, magma heats it. The hot water mixes with **minerals** to create **hydrothermal** fluid. This fluid shoots back up through **vents**. Hydrothermal vents and other parts of the seafloor are challenging to study. Ocean engineers design deep-sea vessels and sampling tools to help scientists explore them.

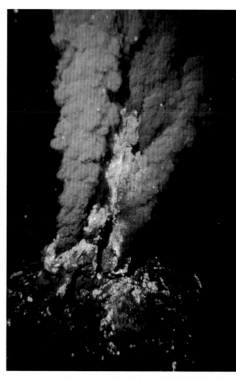

Hydrothermal fluid shooting through a vent looks like smoke when it hits cold ocean water.

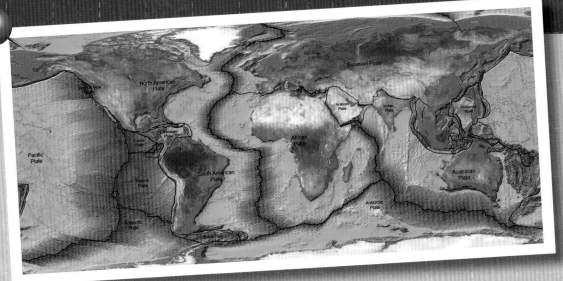

Mid-ocean ridges (marked in red) connect to form the longest mountain range on Earth. It is close to 37,000 miles (60,000 km) long.

Ocean cross-section

Ocean zones are stacked layers with different depths and characteristics. Ocean engineers design **submersible** cameras, sensors, and other tools that work well in the specific conditions of each area.

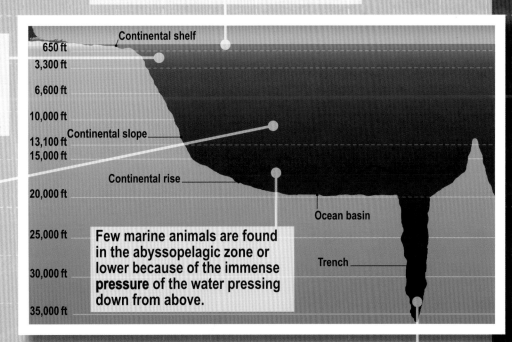

The epipelagic zone is the warmest, sunlit layer. Winds move the waters in this layer. It is home to most marine mammals.

The mesopelagic zone has less light as it gets deeper. The greatest temperature drop occurs in this zone.

The bathypelagic zone is home to **bioluminescent** animals. Their bodies provide the only light.

Few marine animals are found in the abyssopelagic zone or lower because of the immense **pressure** of the water pressing down from above.

Continental shelf
650 ft
3,300 ft
6,600 ft
10,000 ft
Continental slope
13,100 ft
15,000 ft
Continental rise
20,000 ft
Ocean basin
25,000 ft
Trench
30,000 ft
35,000 ft

The hadalpelagic zone is in the trenches at plate boundaries. These are the deepest, coldest, and saltiest parts of oceans. The pressure in this zone is equal to a person holding 50 large airplanes!

OCEANS IN MOTION

Ocean engineering designs must take into account the constant movement of water. This movement is caused when energy transfers to the water from some other source, such as the wind. It blows on an ocean's surface and meets resistance that causes waves. Stronger winds create larger waves.

A powerful wave forms in the Pacific Ocean off the coast of Hawaii.

Underwater earthquakes and volcanic eruptions also send energy through ocean waters. The giant waves that form may become tsunamis. The height of the water rises above sea level as a tsunami speeds toward land.

Tidal waves occur in coastal areas. These waves get their energy from the push and pull of the Sun and Moon's **gravity** and Earth's rotation. High and low tides follow predictable patterns each day.

OCEAN CURRENTS

Waves cause ocean waters to rise and fall. In contrast, **currents** are in constant motion under water. They flow like rivers in one direction and can travel around the world. One kind of current moves just below the water's surface. Winds are the major cause of these currents. A different kind of current created by tides follows the same patterns as high and low tide. Tidal currents are most powerful in coastal areas.

Changing salt levels and temperatures in ocean zones produce a third kind of ocean current. This slower-moving but strong current carries huge amounts of water in massive circles through oceans. This movement is the "global conveyor belt." It spreads around **nutrients** and controls temperatures in oceans.

Ocean water on the global conveyor belt takes about 1,000 years to move around the world.

Current meters such as this measure the speed of water movement in oceans.

Engineering solutions: Some engineers develop ways to study the movements of ocean waters. For example, current meters collect information about water currents. Engineers may use this data to improve designs for other projects. Ocean currents and waves can be very powerful. They are strong enough to damage or carry away ocean engineering technologies. Understanding the currents and waves helps engineers create effective moorings, such as buoys to hold technologies in place in ocean waters. Ocean engineers also design underwater foundations that withstand currents.

Offshore oil and gas rigs are huge structures that need to be built with stable underwater foundations.

WHAT'S IN THE WATER?

If you filled a clear container with water from the ocean, what do you think you might see? It is unlikely you would see much at all, except water. However, ocean water contains powerful things the human eye cannot detect. They can destroy technologies developed by ocean engineers. Two of the major challenges that engineers consider during the design process are salt levels and tiny sea life called bacteria.

BACTERIA

Most sea life lives in zones where sunlight makes **photosynthesis** possible. Fewer nutrients mean less diversity of life forms in lightless zones. Some creatures thrive there, however. Hydrothermal fluid shoots from vents and warms the water around them. This creates warm, nutrient-rich homes for bacteria. They often live in the same hotspots on the seafloor that ocean scientists want to observe and learn more about.

The bacteria can cover and clog parts of submersible vessels, which are vehicles that operate under water. Ocean engineers call this damage biofouling. It affects many ocean technologies. Devices that stay near hydrothermal vents for long periods are at greater risk than when they are in colder ocean waters.

Bacteria and tube worms, such as the ones shown above, live together near hydrothermal vents. Bacteria make their homes on the tube worms, which then absorb the bacteria.

Shellfish called barnacles are a common cause of biofouling.

Salinity: Why is ocean water saltier than water found inland? It starts with **carbon dioxide** in the air, which mixes with rain. When this rain falls on rocks, it causes them to wear away. The small, broken rock particles include salty minerals that dissolve in rainwater. They flow along with the rain into waterways and eventually oceans. Sea life consumes some of the salts. The rest remains in the ocean, which makes it salty. Eruptions from underwater volcanoes also add a small amount of salty minerals into oceans.

Salinity is the amount of salt found in water. Salt speeds up corrosion in metal vessels, devices, and structures. Corrosion is a natural chemical process that weakens and breaks apart metals. Ocean engineers look for construction materials and coatings that resist corrosion. They must also understand salinity because it affects how objects float in water (see pages 20 and 21.)

Bacteria feed on the corroded metal of a shipwreck. They also eat underwater ocean engineering designs that are made from metal.

HISTORICAL TECHNOLOGIES

More than 200 scientists and crew members worked together on the HMS Challenger.

Research ships using low-tech solutions made the earliest discoveries about the ocean depths. In 1868, the British survey ship HMS *Lightning* found deep-sea life at 14,400 feet (4,389 m). A scouring device attached to a long towline collected samples. From 1872 to 1876, the HMS *Challenger* expedition made several breakthroughs. Using tools such as cables to touch the seafloor, the crew discovered the Mid-Atlantic Ridge and outlined the shapes of ocean basins. They also found the world's deepest ocean trench—now named Challenger Deep.

It was a tight fit for the crew inside the Triste submersible!

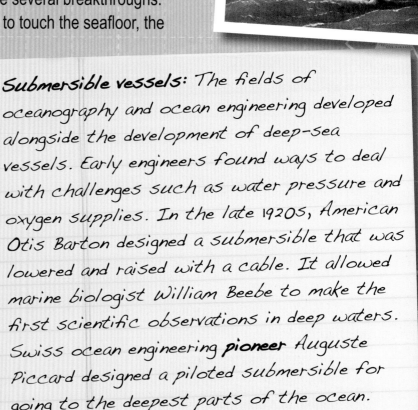

Submersible vessels: The fields of oceanography and ocean engineering developed alongside the development of deep-sea vessels. Early engineers found ways to deal with challenges such as water pressure and oxygen supplies. In the late 1920s, American Otis Barton designed a submersible that was lowered and raised with a cable. It allowed marine biologist William Beebe to make the first scientific observations in deep waters. Swiss ocean engineering **pioneer** Auguste Piccard designed a piloted submersible for going to the deepest parts of the ocean. In 1960, his son Jacques and a U.S. Navy lieutenant tested Trieste, the third version of his machine. They made history by taking it to the bottom of Challenger Deep, a depth of around 36,000 feet (11,000 meters).

SONAR

The sinking of the RMS Titanic after it struck an iceberg in 1912 highlighted the need to detect unseen objects in the ocean. Canadian Reginald Fessenden created one of the first devices to pick up underwater echoes bouncing off icebergs. Soon after, navies developed sound navigation and ranging (sonar) devices. Sonar helped them detect submarines under water. While passive sonar listened for sounds made by objects such as submarines, active sonar transmitted a short burst of sound energy that reflected off an object and produced an echo. Echoing **sound waves** move more easily through water than through air. This remote sensing technology helped create images of what was not visible under water.

In the 1960s, the U.S. Navy developed a sonar system that sent out rapid sounds. It created images showing depths in rainbow colors. Engineers continue to improve on this technology today.

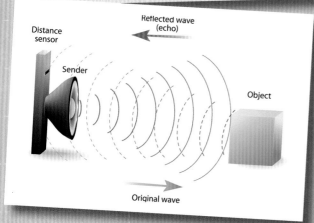

Active sonar sends sound waves outward. The waves bounce off underwater objects and return to the sensor, which receives data.

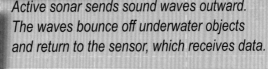

JACQUES COUSTEAU

Have you ever imagined yourself as an explorer, heading off to find undiscovered lands? Filmmaker Jacques Cousteau was like that. But instead of hiking unexplored mountains, he decided to plunge into the depths of the ocean. In 1930, Cousteau began naval training in his homeland of France. It was then that he grew a passion for reaching inaccessible underwater locations. One of his contributions to ocean exploration was the Aqua-Lung. He **collaborated** with French engineer Emile Gagnan to develop this early diving gear. In the 1960s, Cousteau's team created an underwater base camp. It allowed "oceanauts" to spend weeks living in and observing the ocean.

Jacques Cousteau explored oceans using a variety of ocean technologies, including this submersible diving saucer.

MODERN OCEAN ENGINEERS

Are you able to solve complex problems? Can you share your ideas and work well in a team setting? If so, ocean engineering might be a good fit for you. Ocean engineers need a solid understanding of computers, math, and science. Knowledge of oceans is necessary, too. Other kinds of engineers may also work on ocean-related projects. In fact, ocean engineering combines many fields, including civil, electrical, and mechanical engineering. Engineers often team up with other professionals. For example, they work with technicians who build and operate ocean engineering designs. They also collaborate with oceanographers.

Ocean engineers use their training and skills in different ocean-based settings. Here are some of the most common areas where you will find ocean engineers at work:

Offshore structures: These structures include oil platforms and rigs for drilling into the seafloor. Ocean engineers provide solutions for dealing with the impacts of wind and waves on these structures. They also help other engineers design strong moorings and foundations in oceans. For example, ocean engineers are part of teams installing ocean-based wind turbines that provide clean and **renewable** energy.

Ocean engineers collaborate with people working on offshore structures to study the effects of waves and currents. Their research helps them with future designs.

Dr. Stefan Williams designed the remotely operated vehicle (ROV) launching in the background here. One of its tasks was looking for signs of global warming around the Great Barrier Reef off the coast of Australia.

Exploration tools: Ocean exploration requires many different tools. Some engineers develop devices that collect or track data about ocean life. Consulting with scientists who use ocean technologies, engineers may also design vessels for use in the deep sea. Some have human crews. Others are remotely operated vehicles (ROVs) or robotic, self-driving **autonomous** underwater vehicles (AUVs).

Natural resources: Ocean engineers also create solutions for harvesting or protecting natural resources. For example, some engineers may design ways to find and remove minerals such as gold, copper, and silver from seafloors. Others may develop the tools needed to investigate potential new energy sources such as hydrothermal vents. Innovative ideas that limit marine pollution are a further area of focus.

SHIP DESIGN

Ocean engineering is a broad field, but it rarely includes ship design. Naval architects develop plans for new ships. They work with marine engineers, who create and maintain the mechanical equipment used on ships.

START WITH A PROBLEM

Most ocean engineering projects involve large teams of people with different skills. This is the case at Woods Hole Oceanographic Institution (WHOI). This American ocean research and education facility is in the state of Massachusetts. In the early 1990s, a team at WHOI knew they had a problem. They kicked off an engineering design process that led to a solution.

Alternatives to Alvin: For decades, WHOI had been exploring the ocean using a submersible vessel called Alvin. Its design allowed scientists to travel safely to the abyssopelagic zone. However, running it cost up to $40,000 a day. Half of the time, scientists returned to sites they had visited before, so that they could observe any changes. Barrie Walden, who oversaw these missions, thought it was time for an innovative, less costly way to conduct this follow-up research. This would save Alvin for missions that justified the high cost of using it. He challenged a group of WHOI engineers and scientists to solve this design problem.

Alvin *returns to the surface after a dive. The vessel was developed in the 1960s. WHOI upgrades Alvin every few years, so all the original parts were replaced a long time ago.*

16

Researching details

After defining the challenge, the next step in the engineering design process is to research the details of the task. Ocean engineers consider the criteria for success. These are the needs of the final design, such as function, performance, and safety. They also research information that helps them work within the project's constraints (limits). Constraints include the budget and only using materials that will hold up well in the ocean.

Some submersible vessels are designed to descend to great depths, where the water is extremely cold and salty.

Criteria and constraints: Ocean engineer Al Bradley and his WHOI team came up with a long list of criteria. For example, the vessel had to be capable of surveying the seafloor at the same depth as Alvin. The craft also needed to maneuver well and be stable in the deep sea. Constraints on the solution included the size, shape, and weight of the vessel. It had to meet the specifications for storage and launching on a variety of research ships. The materials had to hold up to the cold, salinity, pressure, and currents in the abyssopelagic zone. Another limiting factor was the funding.

POSSIBLE SOLUTIONS

After researching a problem, ocean engineers brainstorm as many ideas as possible. Moving forward with every option would take up too much time and resources. Instead, they decide which one most closely meets their criteria and constraints. After brainstorming and narrowing down to one idea, ocean engineers begin making a **prototype**. They sketch designs, prepare computer models, and build physical prototypes for use in the testing stage.

Brainstorm ideas: The WHOI team came up with ideas for new kinds of underwater surveying vehicles that could replace the expensive Alvin submersible. They brainstormed ideas for smaller ROVs and AUVs (see page 15) that did not need human crews. Without the need for life-support systems, the submersible would be less expensive to build and run. With no people onboard, it could also stay longer under water. The team wondered: What roles would human operators play? Could they program a device to collect data from the ocean on its own? Asking questions is a great way to get ideas flowing.

When ocean engineers brainstorm as a group, they challenge one another to come up with new and creative ideas.

Select a solution: After considering many questions and ideas, the WHOI team selected an idea that they thought might work. They chose to develop a self-driving vessel that could dive to the seafloor and collect data about marine life, landforms, and processes. Its preprogrammed movements would be similar to a lawnmower traveling back and forth in straight lines. The unmanned craft would not need to return to the surface as often as Alvin did with its human crew. Instead, the new design could survey in warm water, then "sleep" in a cold spot with less bacteria in it. This move would prevent biofouling (see pages 10-11), which could reduce the need for costly maintenance.

Build a prototype: After working out the design details on paper and in computer models, the WHOI team built a prototype to move forward to the testing stage. They called it the Autonomous Benthic Explorer—or ABE for short. It was triangular with three torpedo-shaped pods. The team thought this design would keep it stable and help stop it from drifting too much in strong currents. The top two pods contained most of the materials that made ABE float. Heavier equipment went in the pod underneath. Five propellers moved it up, down, forward, and backward like a helicopter. They could attach various tools, such as cameras, depending on its mission.

Models of ABE filled ocean engineer Al Bradley's workshop.

BUOYANCY

Many ocean engineering devices float on or hover in water. The **force** of gravity pulls them down toward the seafloor. The **buoyant** force of liquid pushes them back toward the surface. **Buoyancy** can also refer to an object's ability to float. When the **density** of the object is less than the density of the water, it floats on the surface of the water. This is positive buoyancy. If the densities are equal, neutral buoyancy occurs and the object hovers in the water. If the density of the object is greater than the density of the water, the object sinks. This is negative buoyancy.

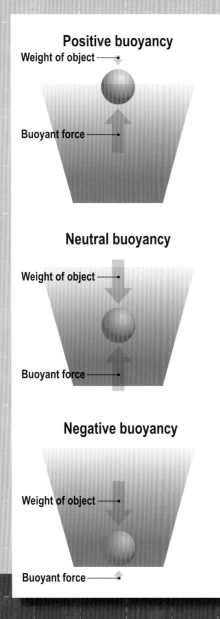

Positive buoyancy
Weight of object

Buoyant force

Neutral buoyancy
Weight of object

Buoyant force

Negative buoyancy
Weight of object

Buoyant force

ABE's buoyancy
Ocean engineers must consider salinity when they design for buoyancy. High levels of salt in water increase its density. This gives the water more buoyant force. The ABE design team addressed this during the prototype stage. They developed weights and floats that would change the explorer's buoyancy in the salty ocean waters. Hollow glass balls in its upper pods gave ABE positive buoyancy. Small, heavy weights attached to its body helped it sink to the desired depth. When the descent weight detached, the vessel's overall density decreased and it became neutrally buoyant. To return to the surface, ABE dropped a second weight and floated to the surface.

Can you think of examples for each level of buoyancy? What kinds of objects sink, float, or hover in water?

This device is neutrally buoyant while it collects small particles from the ocean. It stops hovering and returns to the ocean's surface after its mission is complete.

TRY IT YOURSELF!

Are you ready to experiment with buoyancy? First, gather the following supplies:

- whole, unpeeled orange
- large, clear pitcher of water
- box of table salt
- large spoon
- paper and pen for noting observations

Do you think the peel will make the orange more or less buoyant? Place the unpeeled orange in the water and watch what happens. Next, peel the orange. Return it to the water and observe any changes in buoyancy. Did you observe the results that you expected? How did the air trapped under the peel affect the orange's density? To simulate ocean water, pour one spoonful of salt into the water. Stir the water to help the salt dissolve. Keep adding salt and stirring until the orange has positive buoyancy again. Note how the increase in salinity changes the buoyant force of the water.

TEST AND REFINE

After building a prototype, ocean engineers plan and conduct tests for it. They collect and evaluate the test results. Engineers do not expect their first prototypes to function perfectly. They study any setbacks, as well as what worked well. Then they use what they learn to improve their designs.

Test the prototype: The WHOI team first tested their ABE prototype off a dock in Woods Hole Harbor on the Atlantic coast. They needed to partner with a research crew to test it in deeper waters. However, most scientists did not think ABE would ever be useful to them. It was difficult to persuade anyone to test it on a deep-sea expedition. Finally, a research mission agreed to test ABE. Its first dive was in 1994. It went down 13,450 feet (4,100 m) to the seafloor. Unfortunately, it could not release its diving weight. ABE was stuck until Alvin rescued it. The team dealt with this design flaw and others in the next step of the design process.

Al Bradley (left) tries out ABE in a test well at Woods Hole Harbor.

The improvement stage allows ocean engineers to fix problems they found during testing. After they refine the prototype, they test it again. They also make **trade-offs**. For example, moving at high speeds may be useful in a submersible vessel, but conserving battery power is more important. The design might change so it uses less power, even if it means the vessel moves slower. Engineers continue to improve the prototype until it works as well as it can. This process is called **optimization**. If the first possible solution does not work, engineers return to the earlier steps in the design process to do more research and try other ideas.

Improve the design: After the first deep-sea test of ABE failed, the WHOI team refined parts of its design, including the diving weight's release system. The following year, a second scientific research trip agreed to retest ABE on the open ocean (above). They reported that it worked surprisingly well as a surveying tool. The team was eager to test it again. However, they did not have enough funding and the project stalled for several years. Finally, WHOI collaborated with the National Oceanic and Atmospheric Administration (NOAA) to finish ABE. This partnership also allowed them to upgrade parts such as ABE's batteries, **navigation system**, and sonar.

As ocean engineers develop solutions, they consider any negative effects their designs may have on ocean environments. They must balance the rewards of making new discoveries against risks such as disturbing marine life.

SHARE SOLUTIONS

The design process concludes with engineers telling the story of their process. They share the details with other engineers and the world through conferences and **journals**. After the engineering design process concludes, the prototype may go into production.

Share the solution: WHOI shared information about ABE's completed design with ocean engineers and scientists. Reports and presentations described their process and results. Its design inspired a new generation of unmanned submersibles. The expensive prototype became operational. It used durable, corrosion-proof materials that allowed for deep-sea testing, which meant it could stay in use.

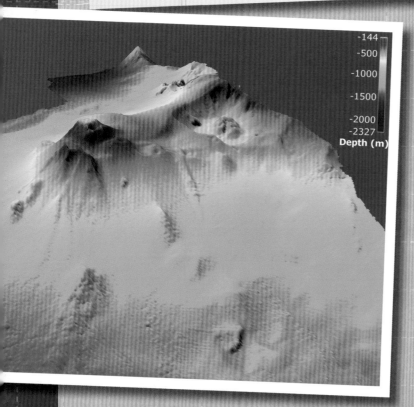

Depth (m)
-144
-500
-1000
-1500
-2000
-2327

ABE in action

In 1999, ABE found hydrothermal vents in the East Pacific Rise mid-ocean ridge. Without this ocean engineering technology, they may not have been discovered. With many scientists eager to study hydrothermal vents, searching for them became ABE's focus. WHOI upgraded ABE's cameras to capture finer details. It was the first AUV to provide detailed maps of mid-ocean ridges at the boundaries of tectonic plates.

ABE made detailed maps of the seafloor that showed landforms such as underwater volcanoes.

ABE worked overnight preparing seafloor maps, so they were ready for scientists to use in the mornings. New programming gave ABE the ability to analyze data, which helped it find more vents.This information helped scientists further their study of the seafloor. Its discoveries gained worldwide attention. In 2006, *Wired* magazine named ABE one of the 50 Best Robots Ever. They said, "Mars may belong to the rovers, but the oceans belong to the Autonomous Benthic Explorer."

INTRODUCING SENTRY

On March 5, 2010, a research ship off the coast of Chile lost contact with ABE. After more than 200 successful dives, it disappeared in the deep sea. A crack in a glass flotation ball may have caused it to shatter. At great pressure, the released air would have the same power as three sticks of dynamite. The fate of the Autonomous Benthic Explorer is still unknown. Its loss highlights the challenges of working in the ocean. In the early 2000s, ABE's design team started working on a new AUV design called Sentry. It had improved speed, control, and operating time. It took over the work of ABE.

The design process for Sentry *took several years. These WHOI engineers tested it in the ocean in 2007.*

DESIGN CHALLENGE

It's time to put what you have read into practice! Remember that ocean engineers often work in teams. Consider inviting a friend to help you with this design challenge. Follow each step to develop a submersible vessel that can switch from positive to neutral buoyancy. Make the challenge tougher by designing a way to change the buoyancy without putting your hands in the water. Choose waterproof materials—here are a few ideas to get you started:

- objects such as sports balls, plastic drink bottles with caps, and wooden craft sticks

- weights such as magnets, marbles, and rocks

- duct tape, glue, elastic bands, and other supplies to connect parts

You will also need a space for testing. This could be a sink, a bathtub, or even a pool if you have adult supervision. Get creative and explore multiple solutions. You may need to make trade-offs to optimize your design.

1. Define your task: Make sure you understand your challenge. Flip back to pages 20 and 21 to review the basics of buoyancy. Explain positive and neutral buoyancy in your own words.

2. Investigate: What are your criteria and constraints? Your design needs to be able to float and hover in water. The size of your test space will limit the size of your design.

3. Brainstorm: Brainstorm plenty of ideas for your vessel. In your own experience, have you seen objects with positive or neutral buoyancy? What materials would be easy to attach and remove so your design will hover and float? Develop the ideas you think are most likely to work.

4. Select an idea: Compare your ideas to your list of criteria and constraints. Which solution do you think fits well with your needs and limits? Choose the idea that you think is the best one to develop first.

5. Build: Start by making detailed sketches of your design. They will help you picture your idea, the materials you need, and how parts may connect. After your plans are complete, construct your prototype. The first version may not be perfect! You can optimize it during later stages.

6. Test: Place your prototype in water and observe its buoyancy. Did it hover or float when it was supposed to? Without making changes to the design, repeat the test. Note your results and observe if there are any differences from the earlier trial.

When a submarine releases water held in tanks, the vessel becomes more buoyant and rises to the surface.

7. Improve: Based on your results, list the pros and cons of your prototype. What changes do you think you need to make to your design? Remember, density affects buoyancy. One way to alter buoyancy is to change the shape of the object, so the mass is spread over more or less space. Make your improvements and test it again. If your design still isn't working the way you want it to, you might decide to develop a different idea.

8. Share: After you optimize your design, share your process and results. Present your findings to a friend, your classmates, or a family member. Ocean engineers share their work using diagrams and written descriptions. You could also prepare a video or live representation to report on your process.

FUTURE OF THE FIELD

The oceans hold many natural resources that could help humans in the future. For example, energy moving through tidal waters or coming from hydrothermal vents is renewable and does not cause pollution. Ocean engineers help design ways to study and use these potential energy sources. Innovative ideas allow for the collection of more detailed data. Other ocean engineers play a role in ensuring the world's shared marine resources are not overused. This includes designing tools to observe and monitor human impact on the oceans.

This technology in the Atlantic Ocean off the coast of Portugal converts the motion of waves into electricity.

DETECTION AND WARNING

Some ocean engineers will help save lives in the future by designing ocean-based devices that sense upcoming natural hazards, such as earthquakes, tsunamis, and extreme weather. These tools are part of an expanding global system for detecting such threats. This kind of system gave some people a warning approximately one minute before the Great East Japan Earthquake in 2011. This was enough time to stop things such as moving trains and surgeries in progress, but more notice could have saved thousands of lives. Ocean engineers are pioneering new ways to study and monitor underwater hazards. These may lead to earlier warnings before disasters strike.

This tsunami-detecting device was launched into the South China Sea.

The Perdido oil and gas rig in the Gulf of Mexico has decks that are each the size of two football fields. It weighs more than 60,000 tons (54,400 metric tons!)

Improving offshore structures: Offshore structures do not last in the same way as structures on land. Ocean constructions are rarely more than 30 years old. Sometimes they become corroded and weak in their ocean settings. In other instances, they are no longer needed. The owners of drilling rigs and energy platforms are responsible for dismantling them. Taking them apart and removing the pieces from the ocean is difficult and expensive. It can also harm nearby marine life. Some ocean engineers look for more environmentally friendly solutions. One option is to reuse the structures as artificial reefs or scientific observatories. Another idea for the future is to find a way to put metal-eating bacteria to work. Ocean engineers also develop designs for new offshore structures that are easier to dismantle.

Old offshore structures can be developed into artificial reefs that create shelters for marine life.

LEARNING MORE

BOOKS

Mara, Wil. *Deep-Sea Exploration: Science, Technology, Engineering.* Children's Press, 2015.

Medina, Nico. *Who Was Jacques Cousteau?* Grosset & Dunlap, 2015.

Peppas, Lynn. *Ocean, Tidal, and Wave Energy.* Crabtree, 2009.

Pratt, Mary K. *Exploring Under the Sea.* ABDO Publishing, 2014.

Sheehan, Robert. *The Undersea Lab: Exploring the Oceans.* Powerkids, 2014.

Spilsbury, Louise, and Richard Spilsbury. *Robots Underwater.* Gareth Stevens, 2015.

Woodward, John. *Ocean: A visual encyclopedia.* Dorling Kindersley, 2015.

ONLINE

www.amnh.org/education/resources/rfl/web/findavent/
Visit this American Museum of Natural History site to learn about hydrothermal vents in the Find a Vent activity.

www.divediscover.whoi.edu/index.html
Get details about 15 ocean expeditions and more at WHOI's Dive and Discover: Expeditions to the Seafloor site.

http://ocean.si.edu/deep-sea
Find plenty of information on oceans and technology at the Ocean Portal run by the Smithsonian National Museum of Natural History.

www.coexploration.org/oe/kws/start.html
Explore ocean life, landforms, and technologies at NOAA's My Submarine: Ocean Explorer interactive website.

www.youtube.com/watch?v=mL-FzBUAHuQ
Watch Dr. Kate Moran describe deep ocean processes and materials.

PLACES TO VISIT

ExplorOcean, Newport Beach, California: The hands-on exhibits at this educational facility and marina include the Ocean Literacy Center, a makerspace, and an ocean innovation lab.
http://explorocean.wpengine.com

Woods Hole Oceanographic Institute, Woods Hole, Massachusetts: Tour the facilities and harbor where ABE and many more ocean engineering solutions were developed.
www.whoi.edu/visitus

GLOSSARY

autonomous Controls itself

bioluminescent Describes life forms that produce light from their bodies

buoy An object that floats on the surface of water and is secured to the ground or a weight under water

buoyancy A liquid's ability to make an object float or an object's ability to float

buoyant Makes objects float or is able to float

carbon dioxide A gas that humans and animals breathe out or is the result of burning fuels

collaborate To work together

current A body of water or air moving in a definite direction

density Mass (amount of material) of an object per unit of volume (space the object takes up)

force The push or pull on an object

gravity A force that pulls any two objects (masses) toward each other; for objects on Earth, the result of gravity is a downward force, toward the center of the planet.

hydrothermal Related to hot water that is usually warmed by magma

journal A magazine in which professionals who are focused on a particular field share information and the results of their work

magma Hot, melted rock that is found beneath Earth's crust

minerals Solid materials that are the main ingredients of rock and soil

navigation system Interconnected parts that work together to plot a route

nutrient A substance that living things need to function

observatory A specially designed structure used by scientists to observe the natural world

optimization Improvement in a design to make it function as well as possible

photosynthesis A process in which green plants use sunlight to make food

pioneer The first person who develops an idea or technique

pressure The amount of force or weight that pushes against an area of another object

prototype An early model of a design built to test the design's function

renewable Describes an energy source that cannot be depleted or used up

sensor A part of a system that collects information from its surroundings

sound waves Vibrations that travel in all directions through substances, but which won't go through empty space

submersible Usable under water

technology A machine or tool created by engineers or scientists to solve problems

tectonic plates Moving top layers of Earth's crust

trade-off A circumstance in which one criterion is set aside

tsunami A huge ocean wave caused by natural hazards such as earthquakes under the ocean

vent An opening through which liquid or gas escapes

INDEX